Amazing Fish
of the World

LEVEL **2** READER

READING LEVEL
GRADES 1 TO 3

Written by Kathryn Knight
Illustrated by Edizioni Larus S.p.A.

Franklin, Tennessee 37068-2068. 1-866-418-2572.
No part of this book may be reproduced or copied in any form without written permission
from the copyright owner. CE12665/1011

Everywhere Fish!

Fish swim in all the waters on Earth—the salty oceans and seas and the fresh waters of lakes, ponds, and rivers. Not all animals that live in water are fish. Many are mammals, such as seals, dolphins, and whales. Others are

Monk Seal

Starfish

Seabream

Grouper

Seahorse

Octopus

Moray Eel

reptiles, such as turtles, sea snakes, and alligators. Octopuses, starfish, coral, and shellfish are not fish. Most fish have fins, gills, bones, and scales, but not all. Seahorses have bones but no scales. Sharks have fins and gills but no bones or scales (they have "skin teeth").

Swordfish

Tuna

Blue Shark

Sea Turtle

Sole

Brittle Star

Barnacles

Rainbow Wrasse

Sharks

The largest fish are the sharks. Sharks are able to twist and turn easily because they have no bones. Instead they have firm tissue called *cartilage* (like the cartilage that forms your ears).

Great white sharks can grow to 20 feet long and weigh 3,500 pounds. But the biggest fish in the ocean is the whale shark. It can grow to 40 feet and weigh 30,000 pounds. That's a lot of fish!

Tuna

Another giant of the sea is the northern bluefin tuna. There are many types of tuna that swim the oceans of the world, and this is the largest. These tuna can grow to over 12 feet and weigh 1,000 pounds. Tunas are *carnivorous* (meat-eating), feeding on smaller fish.

Sturgeon (STIR-jun)

Sturgeons are the freshwater giants of the fish world. Many live only in lakes and rivers. Others live in the saltier coastal waters or travel between fresh and saltwater. These big fish are bottom-feeders, sucking shellfish and fish into their toothless mouths. The largest sturgeons can grow to over 15 feet and weigh 1,000 to 4,000 pounds.

Marlin

The marlin is one of the racers of the sea. It can zip through water at 60 miles an hour and make amazing leaps at the surface. Marlins are billfish, having a spearlike snout. They can reach 15 to 18 feet and can weigh 1,200 to 1,700 pounds.

Swordfish

Another billfish is the swordfish. Like the marlin, this is a big, speedy fish. Females are larger than males and can weigh over 1,000 pounds.

Swordfish do not use their snout to spear prey. They use their bill to stir up schools of fish to stun them. Then the swordfish can gulp a slow-moving fish into its toothless mouth.

Swordfish do not harm humans. However, hurt swordfish have at times "attacked" small fishing boats.

Atlantic Cod

This big cod is a deepwater fish, swimming along the seafloors of the northern Atlantic. It was such a popular food fish, that there are now very few left. New laws protect this fish, which can grow to 6 feet and weigh close to 200 pounds. Atlantic cods may live for 25 years.

Dusky Grouper

Grouper

There are many kinds of groupers in all oceans of the world. Some, like the dusky grouper, are dull brown. Others are spotted and brightly colored. All have huge mouths that suck in prey with one big gulp.

Miniata Grouper

Groupers are slow-swimming, thick, heavy fish. They can grow to 3 feet and weigh as much as 200 pounds.

Tiger Grouper

Barracuda (Bear-ah-KOO-dah)

One of the fiercest saltwater predators is the barracuda. This fang-toothed fish swims in all the oceans. The largest barracudas can be over 5 feet long. They have razor-sharp teeth that— snap!—easily tear chunks from large prey. The barracuda is called the "Tiger of the Sea."

Most adult barracudas hunt alone. Younger ones may stick together in a *battery* (school of barracudas).

Northern Pike

The "tiger" of freshwater fish is the northern pike (or jackfish). It lives in rivers and lakes across Europe, Russia, and North America. These big, toothy fish can reach 5 feet. You don't want your hand or big toe near one of these creatures. Pikes can lie still for hours and then strike!—with a mouth full of small daggers. Yowch!

Arapaima (air-ah-PIE-mah)

One of the largest freshwater fish in the world is the arapaima of South America. It can grow to over 6 feet and weigh 200 pounds. The arapaima must come to the surface to gulp air, so it is very easy to catch. There are very few of these odd-looking giants left because they have been over-hunted.

Piranha (per-AW-nah)

Another fish of South America is the small but ferocious piranha. A school of piranhas will quickly attack a wounded animal in the water. Within minutes, they will tear the animal to shreds with their sharp teeth. All that will be left is the animal's skeleton.

Paddlefish

The waters of the Mississippi River are home to the paddlefish. This strange fish can grow to be quite large—up to 5 feet. Its paddle-snout is able to sense small water-creatures, which the fish likes to eat.

Porcupinefish

The porcupinefish is also called a blowfish. It is able to make itself larger (and rounder) by gulping water. If a predator keeps after it, its spiny scales will pop up—like a porcupine's quills. Ouch!

Bowfin (BOE-fin)

The bowfin lives in lakes and rivers of eastern North America. This fish has been around since the days of the dinosaurs. It is the male bowfin that watches over the eggs in a mud nest and protects the *fry* (baby fish) when they hatch.

Gar

Like the bowfin, the North American gar is a freshwater fish that has been around for millions of years. Most gars are about 2 feet long, but the alligator gar can grow to 9 feet.

Lesser Weever

The lesser weever lives in warm seas. It buries itself in the sand and waits for prey. If another fish tries to bite it, the lesser weever has a surprise. The long spine of its *dorsal* (back) fin injects a painful poison!

Sole

The sole starts out like most fish, with an eye on either side of its head. As the sole grows, it flattens out. Its two eyes and mouth "move" to one side of its body. It then can lie flat on the seafloor and, like the weever, hide under the sand.

Wrasse (RASS)

Wrasses live in the shallow waters of oceans and seas. They come in many sizes.

Many, such as the rainbow wrasse, are brightly colored. Most are small, but the humphead wrasse can reach 8 feet and weigh over 300 pounds.

The male cuckoo wrasse can change its coloring, but the females are even more amazing. If there are no males around, some females will change and become male!

Cuckoo Wrasse

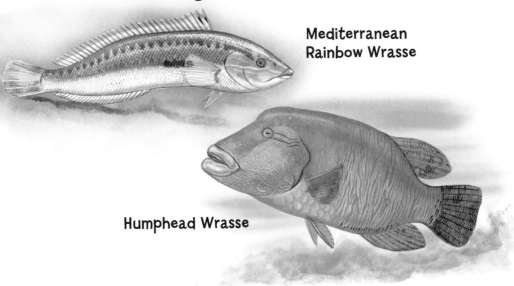

Mediterranean
Rainbow Wrasse

Humphead Wrasse

Sailfin Surgeonfish (SIR-jun-fish)

Surgeonfish (also called tangs) have small spines at the base of the tail. These spines are razor-sharp and can cut a predator. The beautiful sail-like fins give this surgeonfish its name.

Harlequin Filefish

Like surgeonfish, filefish often live in the shallow waters of coral reefs. The long snout helps them reach into coral to eat the soft living part inside. The skin of a filefish is rough, like a fingernail file.

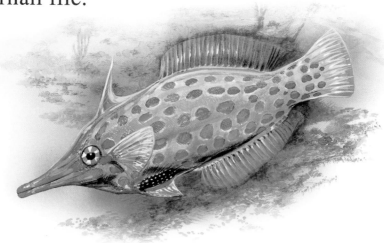

Archerfish

Archerfish are expert marksmen. These fish can shoot a jet of water droplets at an insect sitting on a plant. This knocks the insect into the water where it is gobbled up. Archerfish almost always hit their target on the first try. They can also leap from the water and grab their prey.

Salmon (SAM-un)

Most salmon are born in the clear water of a running stream. After a few years, salmon head downriver until they reach the ocean. Here they live for one to five years.

It is their return trip that is truly amazing. Salmon swim with all their might back up the river for hundreds of miles until they find the exact place where they were born. Sometimes they leap up waterfalls to keep going upstream! Most will die after this long struggle back home. But not until they have carefully laid their eggs—for the cycle to begin again.

Mudskipper

Most fish will not survive long out of water. But a few fish spend some of their time on land. The mudskipper is a fish, but it acts like a frog. It can breathe through its skin and "skip" about on the sand looking for food.

Climbing Perch

Climbing perches can't breathe through their skin. However, using their gills, fins, and tail, these fish can climb out of the water at night and move over land from pond to pond.

Coelacanth (SEE-la-kanth)

This odd-looking fish died out long ago and hadn't been on the Earth for 65 million years. At least, that's what people thought. Imagine the surprise in 1938 when fishermen caught one of these 100-pound fish! How exciting to learn that some coelacanths still live in the deep waters off the African coast! They are nicknamed "living fossils."